W9-BUF-396

SAM'S
BOOK

SAM'S
BOOK

DAVID RAY

Wesleyan University Press
Middletown, Connecticut

MIDDLEBURY COLLEGE LIBRARY

ABC 1/11 D

PS
3568
.A9
S2
1987

10/
Am

Copyright © 1968, 1974, 1979, 1987 by David Ray

"In the Gallery Room" (as "At the Nelson"), "The Father," "Thanks, Robert Frost," and "On the Photograph 'Yarn Mill' by Lewis W. Hine" appeared in *The Touched Life,* copyright © 1982 by Scarecrow Press. Reprinted by permission of Scarecrow Press.

Lines from *The Poetry of Robert Frost,* edited by Edward Connery Lathem, copyright © 1969 by Holt, Rinehart and Winston. Reprinted by permission of Holt, Rinehart and Winston.

The following poems first appeared in these books: "For Samuel Cyrus Ray" and "At the Washing of My Son," *Dragging The Main and Other Poems,* published by Cornell University Press; "The Shoelaces" and "In Greece," *Gathering Firewood,* published by Wesleyan University Press; and "In the Evening" and "A Visit to Lloyd in Amana," *The Tramp's Cup,* published by The Chariton Review.

All rights reserved

Some of the poems in this book appeared originally in *Chester H. Jones Foundation National Poetry Competition Winners 1984, Cincinnati Poetry Review, College English, Confrontation, Field, Georgia Review, Greenfield Review, MSS, New Letters, Pebble, Poetry Now, The Poetry Review, The Spirit That Moves Us, Tendril: The Poet's Choice, Syracuse Scholar, Writers Forum.* "On the Photograph, 'Yarn Mill' by Lewis W. Hine" first appeared in *The New Yorker.*

The author is grateful to The Rockefeller Foundation (Bellagio Study and Conference Center), the Virginia Center for the Creative Arts, and the University of Missouri–Kansas City for fellowships and the many supportive courtesies that were of assistance in the writing of this work.

LIBRARY OF CONGRESS CATALOGING-IN-PUBLICATION DATA

Ray, David, 1932–
   Sam's book.
   (Wesleyan poetry)
   I. Title. II. Series.
PS3568.A9S2   1987   811'.52   86–9195
ISBN 0-8195-5170-8 (alk. paper)
ISBN 0-8195-6180-0 (pbk. : alk. paper)

All inquiries and permissions requests should be addressed to the Publisher, Wesleyan University Press, 110 Mt. Vernon Street, Middletown, Connecticut 06457.

Distributed by Harper & Row Publishers, Keystone Industrial Park, Scranton, Pennsylvania 18512.

Manufactured in the United States of America

FIRST EDITION
Wesleyan Poetry

This book is dedicated to
Samuel Cyrus David Ray (1965–1984)
and to all who loved him

Contents

This day on which
The cherry blossoms fell
    Has drawn to its close.
                —CHORA

Do not claim as your own what is his and not
yours. It is given you for a little while, but it was
born of God, beyond time, in the eternity that is
above all ideas or images.
                —MEISTER ECKHART

That which has sprung from heavenly seed
Back to the heavenly realms returns.
                —EPICTETUS

Noir assassin de la Vie et de l'Art,
Tu ne tueras jamais dans ma mémoire
    . . . qui fut mon plaisir et ma gloire!
                —BAUDELAIRE

SAM'S
BOOK

🍁 Praying for Signs
(the Frost providences)

If my mother had known
the countries I was to travel
and the death I was to die
how she would have wept.
——ENGLISH DITTY

The first was not praying,
just leafing a book—the first word,
a title, was "Maple," the wood
of the casket just yesterday.
In the poem, a girl's name.
"Maple is right," but couldn't it be
that both name and the choice
of a boy's casket is right?
The next sign *was* praying,
hoping to know, like a science,
the trembling thumb hooking
more pages apart, looking
as if to the sky, after speaking
the name of that son. And there too
the meaning seemed clear,
for that morning the father
had looked at a dead skunk
on the road, killed
the same night as his son
(the farm woman swore).
Teeming with maggots, fur fine
as a boy's bloodied hair,
the skunk seemed clearly to say
"Here is no pain, just a bone
being cleaned. There's more
of your son, boy in his fresh grave,
in the birch by the roadside."
So the father took back a birch leaf
and heard the fluttering voice
of the wind, sure that his son
was not in the dirt of a road
but in the green of such birches.

And tore off that leaf, proof
of a kind. The next dip
in the book, Book of Frost
sacred as scripture, was "On Going
Unnoticed." Though said
of a coral root
the words seemed to speak further:
As vain to raise a voice as a sigh
In the tumult of free leaves on high.
What are you, in the shadow of trees
Engaged up there with the light and breeze?
which was more or less what
he had asked of his son, lost
more in the birch leaves than in
the maple box covered with sand,
laced high to the topsoil with roses,
carnations, marigolds, mums,
tears of a mother, baby's-breath
she tossed in right where
his true breath exhaled like frost
would have been had the coffin and sand
not been there—aye just where his breath
would have been if new born—
though days late if he went
right away to another one's breast.
Later in the poem a sentence says
(though surely of no reference to
the leaf the father tore and took
back to the farm where goats and cats,
ponies, chickens, dogs maintained
such a home as his boy had loved well):
The only leaf it drops goes wide,
Your name not written on either side.
So much for the subject of "Signs,
looking for," from sky and leaf and stone
found at a stop of the last auto train

on the son's favorite shore, stone
buried for years yet crying out
to go along, to join the boy—
and so it did, dug out by hand in haste,
falling to knees an instinct now,
and the stone born of damp sand
so like the boy in rough and male nobility
that all agreed
it belonged on his grave, had been
cast out by fire and thrown down
for the purpose, with only the need
to add his name, SAM, carved there soon,
that stone forever his though bomb
sail past or earth melt and weep.
Still praying, yet unsated, Dad thumbs
again, finds "Iris by Night"—
could hardly be quite relevant,
but just for hell let's search it through:
And then we were vouchsafed the miracle
That never yet to other two befell
And I alone of us have lived to tell . . .
And we stood in it softly circled round
From all division time or foe can bring
In a relation of elected friends.
True of rainbows as that first
great poet had made quite clear
but also apt and true, precise
if meant to paint for time
how it had been around that open grave,
hands joined, songs sung—"Amazing
Grace"—but first the sand, flowers
thrown until they wove
and laced their way up toward ground,
lifting up, grain by grain,
that tapestry, not tramped by feet
but held like leaf in stone, a pattern

ordained like those found in, say,
stained glass, carpet, pine cone—
and what galaxies fulfill in fire.
That pit was filled with roses,
long-stemmed mums, the baby's-breath
—nettles too and thistles meant
to take the sting of sainthood off
the mangled boy who did outdo
in mischief Huck and Tom although
not one had found in him a hint
of malice, nor was there foe
who nursed his spite, glad
he's gone. Consensus had it,
angel Sam! Caught like millefiore
sold in Italy and works of art
in amber, those petals now hold sand,
and sand holds petals too.
And all are lax within that space,
at rest, with no pain there,
oblong, carved out of earth. All
who knelt together there wrote
his name now sacred in that sand
before topsoil closed on wound anew,
would hold in mind as if seen once
through crystal exactly where
his tossed rose fell, was crossed
with mum, jack-in-pulpit, iris,
gladiolus blue—and weeds, a few.
Yet not explicit, these three signs,
no lucky strike at "Once
by the Pacific"—the great Frost poems—
nor the favorites of that boy—
"Come In" and "Dust of Snow"—
which he had written out, one
on a cypress root, one on a slab,
and now the father thinks

the boy himself was "Dust of Snow,"
what he did to a day so much
like flakes that fell to make
a miracle. And the father knew
how Sam had helped him live,
even to this darkness, though no
flake touched him now.
And still he shopped, like poking
in a Bible. Just one more flip,
to prove it's fool's game, all
such seeking. Your son is dead
as the skunk is dead, flat,
drained, no spirit there, and hair
gone fine like wire in three days, nights.
No bone is plow of noble ship nor
new life elsewhere found more fortunate
by far, if virtues count for aught
in this life or the next.
And that white ash Sam carved
in a school workshop
by happenstance alone turns out
to look like angel wings as two
or three hundred seemed to think
who praised him, wept on Sunday,
said he had touched their lives, and deep.
Yet clearly, angel's wings!
Mere accident, like dips in books
and finding gravestones, skunks,
birch leaves named, and then the text.
Yet one more dip to end
the waste—How 'bout a title
page—BUILD SOIL! Well, hell,
one more—for that's too brief.
This refers to clouds
which had seemed that night
(entering the town, the end

of his road) to be so dark
they were meant to be
Unknowing's shade, opaque. But then
the moon broke through—the eye
of God, a light at last to say
this spot of earth is not forgot
(or so an archaic poet might well
have put it). I had that sign, for sure,
but Frost is on about
The clouds, the source of rain, one stormy night
Offered an opening to the source of dew;
Which I accepted with impatient sight,
Looking for my old skymarks in the blue.
Not much in common—dew and hope.
Read on. *But stars were scarce*
                    in that part of the sky,
And no two were of the same constellation—
No one was bright enough to identify;
So 'twas with not ungrateful consternation,
Seeing myself well lost once more, I sighed,
Where, where in Heaven am I?
                    But don't tell me!
Oh, opening clouds, by opening on me wide.
Let's let my heavenly lostness overwhelm me.
I never meant to quote a poem entire
within my own and yet that night
my son was dead and this small town,
his road's end, had been my destination.
For two days I had flown through air,
moved mountains, so it seemed, to wash
blood off stone. And then I had
that sign, "Lost in Heaven," moon clear
as all our light reflected, Robert's, mine,
Sam's, his sister, all who loved him,
shared his short, good life. And then
his stone, placed before my path,

that birch tree, skunk, and other signs
soft as a dust of snow. No meaning,
just one stone, Frost's lines mere stems
in sand, dulled mums that fade,
yet some fools still seek signs,
clutch books though no voice calls,
not his that always echoed mine:
"I know you do." Next week
in another state, a wedding
in a church, *The Book
of Common Prayer* falls open of its own
to the service as it had been
for Sam who wrote on a cypress root
Frost's poem "Come In"
and said so it speaks through years
"I left the blue door open
                    for you, Dad."

🍁 The Snapshots

Had we known
these few images
were all we'd have of you
we'd have been taking
pictures all the time.
The one I need to forget
—to stop weeping, to live—
is the one in my mind
without looking.

❧ Teaching

If my lessons to him
meant anything at all
I must listen to them now,
for myself. Love
your own body, I told him,
the goodness of it— Let
the love out. Soaping's
a joy, and I towel now
in front of the mirror
where I caught him once
smirking and naked. Smiling's
no sin. Despise
no one, pray for even
the hard-hearted,
even the steel- and rust-
hearted. Dance a jig when you get out
of the pool, turquoise
as a god's eyes,
as a son's, as
a stone's, for even a stone
must be loved,
wished well on its way
through star after star.

❦ In the Gallery Room

Love divides love. And so, my son,
You choose the happy *Dell*
By Constable, a wading cow,
Silvered tree, a stag, old footbridge
Where you want, you say, "to wade
And take a nap."
After a hundred years this scene
Is fine and cold
On your naked, Brancusian feet.
Your favorite painter, you say,
Is John Constable.
But I choose *Low Ebb,*
In dun and lead, with heavy
Heart choose that—where Gustave
Courbet shows folks in fog
Just barely making it,
The storm about to close
Upon them, making sea's mean
Waves and sky all one.
And that is what you save me from—
By saying there too
You'd like
"To wade and take a nap."

1976

🍁 Son

That day at the pool
the little fellow and I
spotted each other
about the same time.
He wore only a white
sailor cap and laughed,
bread in both hands,
waving those chunks
toward me. His mother
was holding him up
and she bent round
and looked deep
into his blue eyes
to inquire why
he was looking
so intently at me,
the foreign man half
a pool's width away,
why he had singled
me out of dozens, all
ages, a fairly big
crowd. Of course
she had no way
of knowing. His eyes
refused to leave mine,
latched on to me,
and he tried to wriggle
out of her arms, to run
toward me. No way
she could have grasped
it, that he
was my son, had been
my naked laughing boy
in another land,
and on the high Atlantic,
age one, swaying

on a deck, the life
preserver's arch hugged
by both arms, an orange wicket
around him, touching
his head, his feet
on salt planks
and a captain's cap
on his head in augury,
and she too mine
now that these mothers
are so young, children
holding children,
daughter holding
dear son laughing,
welkin-eyed, bread
to offer in both fists.

Vence, 1984

❧ The Apple That Fills the Room

What the young are not prepared for
is the apple that fills the room.
That is not how they proceed.
They are not aware that one will grow
and fill the rotten room.
Let it be a yellow
or a red Delicious or one
from another state. Let it be brown
to the core, with a sere leaf
on the stem. Whatever apple
has been brought in
is the apple that will fill the room.
They are hardly prepared to know.

🍂 For Samuel Cyrus Ray 6/6/65

Was that you,
With red veins like Torchman?
The night before your birth I sought
You in a magazine, fishgill and shell ear.
And were those plastic bags
You peered through women, those coronal
Leapings off the sun, like gold
Hair on end, the hair of a mad god?
Blonde or brunette I didn't know her—
But froglegs and taffy cords, I knew you,
Come to life for speaking to. . . .

I rose from your mother as I would rise
From golden fields
And walked out into Portland—
Toward the throbbing mountain beacons—
Deciding what to say to you.
I staggered till rowhouses fell
At my feet and left crystals,
Castles, mists, and the tinkle
Of some temple bell.

And when I returned you were rising,
Freed of all I had known,
Blessed with blindness approaching this
World, rising for the first time
And last to a world
That would be all sweetness and breast.

🍁 At the Washing of My Son

I ran up and grabbed your arm, the way a man
On a battlefield would recognize a long-lost comrade.
You were still wrinkled, and had a hidden face,
Like a hedgehog or a mouse, and you crouched in
The black elbows of a Negro nurse. You were
Covered with your mother's blood, and I saw
That navel where you and I were joined to her.
I stood by the glass and watched you squeal.
Just twice in a man's life there's this
Scrubbing off of blood. And this holy
Rite that Mother Superior in her white starched hat
Was going to deny me. But I stood my ground.
And then went in where for the first time you felt
Your mother's face, and her open blouse.

1965

✿ The Shoelaces

Bending down to tie my son's shoelace
Where he sits in the stroller
In a bar in Spain, I see below me a jumble
Of geologic layers and rivers
Of time: there are the cross-
Bars, holding the miniature and mystical
Cities; there is my own tweed
Sleeve, steel-toed shoes going back
To freight-loading days, and there is
This little man standing up,
Drunk with enthusiasm for a sick world.

1967

🍁 A Polaroid on the Porch

I think he will resist the evil power of the wound
longer than they think.   —TOLKIEN

I thought something was wrong with the film
or the light that struck our porch there in Spain,
up the slope at Santa Eulalia del Rio. Right away
his small curled fist looked a thousand years old
and the perfect imperfection of his life was captured
as in a varnished painting, a thousand seasons gone.
Yet it was only my son in his diapers, the snapshot
turned to bronze, a rust haze upon his world,
something in the yellow air, a blight upon us.
My eyes could not pierce such a mystery, some curse
laid with blessings upon us. "We will kill them
with kindness," the gods have often said, and we
were not the first, not the last. All was there
before us. He lay with eyes pressed shut, sucking
his thumb, a stalwart frog of a son, dreaming
his way back to stars. All was foreseen and we trembled.

🍁 Calabria

Nobody loved us, not enough to beg
us to stay. Is that why we wound up
in Calabria? At night we sat by the fire
and the beaming, ruddy old woman, bandana
on hair, shared out her wine, was proud
of her Americans. What a catch we were
to break bread with—young couple who busted
her bed. She slapped thigh again
and again, and she loved our boy Sam,
who stood naked in the basin and our girl
bella come un angelo. I'd walk in sun
through hills, stop by the tavern, join old
men back from the States, wanting
to die in the shade, so one had told me.
Wine, small wobbly tables, chess, gossip,
then the Mandarin-nailed clerk
in the little Posta told me anew,
Nobody loved us, *niente,* and he was amused
behind bars, waving that scimitar curled,
proving he never worked hard. Contempt
again had crossed ocean. Even that mountainous
Boot shivered at night and we hugged, vowed
to love one another and those two so small,
committed to us. Fireworks shook fields,
distant hills, echoes of wars coming near.

1967

🍁 In Greece

We ignore the barbed wire
from an old war.
The donkeys bray all night.
My son is the first man
to see the holy moon,
the wrinkled sea
that will shipwreck
no St. Paul tonight,
not in this lovely cove,
calm though the rocks protrude
sharp as knives for a martyr.
"It's the right moon," Sam says.
He is my friend.
I lift him high, so high.
A few flowers survive.

1968

🍁 The Temple at Paestum

Son, forgive me if
for a moment when we saw
the temple at Paestum on the sea
I thought the steps worn on
that stone had been
by your ancient feet
which ran before me.

1968

🍁 In the Evening

Where the brambles close round
like a halo and the rough fire of the heart
begins the mother tells her children
listen to the quietness
listen a long time, then you hear
the small fur of the rabbit, the dark
voices of the roses, the feather
listening.

Where the small hands open
into the wilderness the children
with large eyes say they begin
to hear the small fur of the rabbit
the dark voices of the roses, the feather
listening, and the dead
and rusty men who are still growing
toward the light.

Yorkshire, 1968

✿ For My Son

Sam, we took you to one of the best
zoos in the East Riding,
saw scarlet flamingoes, no,
they were flamingo
flamingoes.
And many, many people.
You found a peacock
perched high above you
on his swing, his great harp
spread wide as his cage.
You looked up at him.
"Please, Peacock" you said,
"throw me down a feather."
And that's how you gave me
this feather.

Yorkshire, 1968

Innocents Abroad

ading Mark Twain's *Innocents Abroad* I curse myself
 not being a good caretaker, for not keeping a diary
en we stumbled around those same fabulous places.
was sunny at Paestum and my babes crawled over
 temple. In Venice we didn't even step
o a gondola or try to sing with the gondolier
t I could have at least noted my profound thoughts
 the Bridge of Sighs. We were so afraid sometimes
expensive restaurants that we trembled and ate
idst pigeons or in little *pensiones* not even listed.
ill had a chance then, or at least it is possible
say so. Sam was still in diapers, came down sick
Padua, cried and cried into the darkness,
t somehow next day we lugged him around, admired
otto and Mantegna, took no notes, not of our lives
ling apart, not of the pastel intensities of saints, not
the marriage itself finished not much later on the same
k that wrecked St. Paul's frail boat, a little harbor
ar the city of Rhodes, home to us all one winter,
 do I find scrawled word of the beaches of Spain where I fell
love so stupidly, not a word of the whirlpool
her eyes, *los ojos,* nor did I describe the balls of black sludge
lled from tankers out on the blue sea, how they reminded
 of West Tulsa, when we kids would come in from barefoot walks
d wipe tar from our feet. By the railroad tracks
ar Venice, streets of water Sam loved, we found a worker's
eteria, potato eaters huddled at long tables.
n rode my shoulders in, the way I had my uncle Henry's
en we went, that terrible year, to the church basement soup
chen. And there, far from the tourist attractions,
 had our last supper in Italy among those workmen uncles
o laughed and lifted their glasses, toasting us.
d my blue-booted son—at three a Bronzino portrait, boy
h feather still to be found in the Uffizi—stood on a chair
ding his own with his sister, who this year
ries him with her everywhere, closer than ever, forgetting
hing.

🍁 Statues

Your childhood a fable for fountains—
I sneaked round behind the barn
to get to you. Next time I lifted off
the doghouse roof and made you yell
and run like hell and we wound up
telling the story again about the kids
who went to the store and bought
some cans that were full of *Poison!*
We all yelled, and ran. Then
we played Sardines (they *weren't*
poison). And you got sassy
because you hadn't been It
for three times running. Listen,
show some respect! I'm *L'Ancienne*
and you're just the Younger, and zip
up your buttons and let's once more
play Statues. We'll stay right here,
Yes, stay, don't move, not at all,
right in the middle of the yard.
We'll build a fountain.

❧ The Iowa Farmhouse

Hoghouses, fireflies
compete to be the last image.
Out for the weekend
Sam says, "Dad
why are there two
sunsets, one in town
and one out here?"
"That's just how it is,"
I tell him the truth,
"one for Iowa City
and one for the corn all around."
I hold him on my knee
as Grampa once held me.
He weeps for his mother.
Back in town, I hear,
he weeps for me. How
can I bear it? Together
we must lift two skies
and hold two rainbows up.

❧ The Old Days

Every day just when my mind
was about to start working
I'd say, "I'm dying for a drink."
We'd walk around K Mart,
me leading the boy,
and I thought I was having deep
thoughts. I would gaze at a mop
upended like a Halloween head,
share that while the rock-and-roll
songs made him dance. And he
was learning life, I thought,
in just such a wandering
labyrinthine fashion
under the neon. I was fitting
him out for the plastic world
and kapok and styrofoam
and he climbed into a canoe he desired.
I handed him oars, shoved it along
on the tile floor, ignoring
the clerk. It was ours, not
some store's, or hers, baleful-eyed old
gramma. And we talked, football
over milkshakes. Six-year-old
expert, he toyed with his straw,
licked pink tongues of ice.
On the farm, he said he saw more
than one sunset, first one in town,
then the other. How the hell, I began,
can a man rent a farm, frozen fields,
empty corncribs, barn just a whistle
for winds while confessing good days
are gone, only hulls of life left.
Even then fields were grieving,
crushed stalks under snow while maimed
creatures sought through
land that was mangled, abandoned, bereft.

Autumn again, and I speak to him,
his grief too, sorrow it happened.
He is with me just as he was
when we drove past the river and I saw
how it always would be, junk caught
on shallows, smear of sunset above,
ochre as a priest's robes and a few
hoboes holding out, clawing about
trying to get back to those days
they once had contempt for.
Those with good sense fished
from the bridge in foul waters
          as if they were clear.

🍁 The Night Sam and Wes Stayed
in Their Own Hotel Room

We won't be scared, Sam says,
jumping up and down, in Cyrano
boots,
We're staying in a skyscraper.
Big Sis Realist looks out and says,
Oh no we're not,
this is just three windows on top
and that's not even scraping.
Just once, near midnight, Wes comes
across the hall, whispers:
Sam's real scared, he says
the radiator's a bomb
and it's about to go off
because it's clicking.
Nonsense, I say, nonsense!
At dawn both sleep at last,
young mouths ajar, toes warm
in the sagging bed,
streams of hair joined,
like descent of water
from pillow of stone. Wild bombs
were clicking still.
But they wake. We hug and brag
to have made it through the night.

🍁 The Father

What I did was lead them up
into the bus,
past Mexican ladies, men
seeking jobs in different cities,
grandmothers with parcels
they wanted me to lift
onto the overhead rack.
The two of them settled
into their seats by blued
windows, and I kissed them,
handed them money,
said "Don't forget,
Daddy loves you . . ."
and stood by the station door
swathed in exhaust fumes,
waving, sending another kiss
again and again, oblivious
as one is with lovers,
overcome. I was overcome
for days, wet about the eyes,
not hearing when spoken to.
Keeper of the mint,
engravings, portraits, seals.

🍁 A Visit to Amana

Amana's come to life again
just after billboards. Corridas.
Crossing of water, Aegean,
Atlantic, Judy in my arms
in various Barcelona
rooms, Sam near drowning
in the Court of the Myrtles
at the great Alhambra
where girls of the harem
swam. (A German tourist
fished him out, sans blue
boot, then asked me
for twenty bucks, I said
for my son
you can have it all,
take it all, this car,
this belt, these sun-
glasses. *Nein, danke,
nur zwanzig, danke.*)
And Sam loved to hear
me tell that story.
"Would you, Dad,
have given him your car?"
Now we are land-
locked, having crossed
waters,
bedded down, whispered.
Often we are children.
Ghosts bring their names
to us, we are saying
vows "naked as jaybirds"
and getting in and out
of cars, and so
drive to Amana, westwards.

Iowa, 1970

🍁 Thanksgiving in Sioux City

Chenille bedspread's wide as a plain,
plowed furrow of field. And three kids romp
on the hotel bed. No use playing
Scrabble, reading *Penguin Island,*
a damn dull book, let's face it.
And if being civilized is reading
damn dull books forever then let's give it up
along with beer, TV, old comics
in the glove compartment, nudist
mags for sure. The car that brought us north
is all iced up. We just tramp past its frozen
windows, roof of snow, we and our three kids.
We find a café with chrome chairs, menu
on the wall, white letters stuck in black—then have
our chicken fried, with frenchfries, gravy, peas,
catchup, soda pop, iced tea, cottage cheese
(which all three still call college cheese,
ever looking forward). Sam's in big boots, Wes
is prying from Sapphina's fist some bauble badly needed.
There's grief, we're not sure why—
fear we'll fall apart still further.
Back across the lot we tramp,
more sleet and snow now, wind that makes us bend,
Napoleonic soldiers. Back in the room again
shag rug breathes its dust. Roofs grow dark,
chimneys become white pyramids. Dusk and it's time
to venture out in stockyard air, descend
to billiards at the Y, just Sam and I. He beats
me every time, racks score with glee. Father's
proud of son triumphant, another moment he can keep.
Parting comes at dawn—place them on the bus, then wave.
Blue frosted windows take their palm prints.
Through miles of snow I give my thanks they
even lived while cattle in the fields stand
like statues, frozen breath upon their beards, snow dust
the gentle brush that sweeps our lost white earth.

🍁 The Visit

I'll meet you at the station,
the old LaSalle, hold your sister's hand,
take care, and count the cows.
"Why do you want me to?"
Your small face, in curls,
and a week of this terrible distance,
the ancient grief stirred up.
I pull you close at every chance
and then you're taken, yet again.
The glass upon your picture
throws moonlight off night waters.
All night I work to help you swim.

🍁 How to Be Loved

That lake was where beneath pine panels
Sam caught me reading *How to Be Loved,*
a popular paperback, and asked me
what it said (he never had that trouble).
Main thing, I said, is never care—
People will not love a man who cares,
who shows he sadly needs that love.
Insouciance is best. And Samuel Cyrus laughed.
"Let's get this straight," he said. "You're reading
a book called *How to Be Loved*
that says the main thing is not to care,
and you care enough to read it. I guess
I love you anyhow." And he went on out
to swim and fish and then install
an old radio in my battered Plymouth Valiant.
I hear them still, my radio, my son.

🍁 Ropewalk

The son is weighed
against feathers.
His father turns
the wooden wheel slow
as Samson round
the grim mill. She
in her bonnet
strolls with their girl
of brown shining
hair touching wide planks.
And they live ready
to love in light
slipping through haze,
coiled cord, tunnage,
that ropewalk ensnaring
all who drift there,
braid the frail strands
of their days, twist
cord out of hair.
And yet they hold
nothing though hands
are laced and unlaced,
hot, moist as young
spiders. And what
they grabbed from their days
in the long covered
room we go on
twisting, braiding
the air, clutching the light.

✤ When My Children Left for the Alps

Having so little, I could give them just this—
their first words, which I still held in mind,
his "Help me!" as he waddled in diapers,
trying a doorknob, in Spain, my Sam-son,
on that island together.
And hers, "Where'd he go?" called out when a dog
ran from her as she sat in a cardboard box
on the floor and I stooped to shove her along.
Now they have gone to cold mountains,
I felt it then, feel it now. And think, They do not
need me to gaze sublimely down upon their fine
climb heavenward, Alpine horn behind full blast
in the blinding snow, high hyaline air. Yet
maybe they heard behind them my call, "Love, Dad."

❦ The Witness

Laughter cannot wash
blood off
stones.
Centuries are required.
And rain,
and magic flared
in deeper vessels
than your eyes.

🍁 End of the Road

Under a dark cloud of unknowing
I came into the town, tired
from a journey through three countries
in three days. The moon broke through
as if with a radiant message.
And yet this was the end of the line,
a life that had meant to do much.
And already had, I now think.
Surely that was what the moon
breaking out of that cloud of unknowing
was trying to tell me. Yet I wept,
because it was the end of the road.

✿ Thanks, Robert Frost

Do you have hope for the future?
someone asked Robert Frost, toward the end.
Yes, and even for the past, he replied,
that it will turn out to have been all right
for what it was, something we can accept,
mistakes made by the selves we had to be,
not able to be, perhaps, what we wished,
or what looking back half the time it seems
we could so easily have been, or ought . . .
The future, yes, and even for the past,
that it will become something we can bear.
And I too, and my children, so I hope,
will recall as not too heavy the tug
of those albatrosses I sadly placed
upon their tender necks. *Hope for the past,*
yes, old Frost, your words provide that courage,
and it brings strange peace that itself passes
into past, easier to bear because
you said it, rather casually, as snow
went on falling in Vermont years ago.

❧ On the Photograph "Yarn Mill," by Lewis W. Hine

A boy, age about eleven,
looking just like my son Sam—
same flaxen hair, same cap
I gave him—long-sleeve
shirt tucked in overalls,
standing between iron spinning
mules in a yarn mill, his dirty
right hand touching the machine,
which is huge and black like oil
and no doubt clacking away, stamped
"MASON MACHINE WORKS
PATENT MASS 1903" in a circle
around a nub, like the other,
so that he is caught between
those two great breasts of iron.
His left hand hangs free
and we could still reach out
and pull him safe unto us. Spools
of yarn recede down rows
beyond him as in the mirrors
of a barbershop; the humming
strings look like the innards
of long pianos whose music dins;
the yarn is beaten now by wooden
mallets, then woven—sheared,
combed, dyed—whatever
the boss men say, in North Carolina,
1908. The boy's face, like Sam's,
is trusting, gazes almost amused
at what's before him. This year,
luckily, a horse. Not a yarn
mill. In a dream last night,
I watched my son assemble
the temple of his life as from
a kit (he was named for kings)
and now I see him standing

between those steel machines,
a boy who had no temple,
who could reach out and touch
that cold iron breast,
then knock it off to joke with men.

❧ Scroll

Walking to the funeral some had flowers
in hand, great bunches of them,
and the children brought gifts for him.
Someone had parked an old truck,
rusty fenders, cracked window, bed full
of birch logs, fallen white branches, chunks
all cut up, bark flaking away. I reached in,
scooped out a scroll of that bark,
white but rough like braille to the hand.
It was something to hold while we wept
and those last words were spoken. When others
gave flowers I gave that, sacred runes,
writing in braille on birch parchment curled.

🍁 Burial

Three cars were to meet, not long past dawn,
to drive north for the burial, and the crossroads
lay heavy on slopes, seemed much like the place
Oedipus came upon, same day as Laïus—
And why did I think of that, as if a father
not a son were slain? I had already begun
searching sky and cloud-light for signs, could not
believe that no word would come forth. Fields
were green as England's and I wondered why
we could not have met there without
such a mission. The world was undamaged,
still great nature to share. Yet had earth
not split? At least blue hearse was out of sight.
Caravan of cars could have been
mere picnic or trip to a game. Perhaps
grim event of a dream was transposed
with our pastoral day. At a stop halfway north
I bought ice cream, comics, sodas for those
who still lived. In the rental car's back seat,
the kids sulked, laughed at last at their games—
success in righting their ship. And I knew
they would make it, hoped I would too. Such
is the gift, life renewed, accepting what
they must, great wound scarred over soon or not soon.
Wellness, worth high praise. But my sickness had begun.

🍁 Treasuring the Snapshot

To go about the indifferent city
cradling a snapshot, precious
because it is all that is left,
is not a futility, but simply
a quest for him still, each time
we are broken. It is not
like those girls in *Così*
fan tutte who cup
the lavaliere portrait, coo
to it happy, though his girls
remember him too, treasure
their copies that fade.
Image is all that we have,
shielded by palm, in a place
where we sat with him, empty
chair now. And at home, marks
on a wall, firm in lead pencil
—degrees on a tide gauge—
each level aspired to, etched
as in stone, first
at my thigh, then most years
leaving their marks. Top line
is my man-child. What
shall I do with this wall
where he stood patient and smiled,
tall while the ruler pressed
down his curls? No image
took hold, and thus
like most walls
it takes what we bring,
has nothing to say, and I turn
to the snapshot, the winds,
golden oaks not yet gone
with glut of tears on the sea.

🍁 Neighbors

Neighbors who pretend not
to know—what kind
of neighbors are those?
—who sneak curious glances,
who offer no word of good will.
Some of them work, by the way,
at Hallmark, famous
for greeting us, yet not one
word from them, out
of their mouths or etched
in pastel. I pass them
with children, their strollers or bikes
slowed for riding beside,
and, as I say, the mothers sneak
glances, measure perhaps
my dark envy, how I would wish
theirs dead, to bring my son back.
And there is nothing to say,
nothing to trade
for nothing, not a word
in return for no neighborly word.

🍁 Mom

Everything has two handles, one by which
it may be borne, the other by which it may not.
—EPICTETUS

Sam and Sapphina and Wini and Wes—
Now and then you'd forget, call me Mom
not Dad, and I was always
infinitely flattered—for only a Mom
truly wins love and gets it—
Now, tired of it all I stay home
and midmorning have coffee in a cup
labeled MOM. It has yellow
daisies, bamboo and intertwined
brown leaves, was hand-painted in Georgia,
has a cracked lip. But I sip from it
while the one labeled DAD
has a red sports car on the side
and not even a handle now,
not one I can get hold of. In a way
I was Mom, seldom Dad, and grieve now
as only a Mom could, midmorning.

🍁 Not at All

My sin was too much hope of thee, lov'd boy.
                                    —BEN JONSON

Not at all. Hope of heaven
is what I thank you for
and life laid neatly out
like routes that pilots fly half-
blind. Once a chimney sweeper came
to our inglenook in Wales.
He laid black brushes out on tile,
and you crawled in soot and ash, laughed,
and had to be scrubbed pink that night
till you gleamed with the new-washed hearth.
And so it is with this life, Sam.
You take me where I need to go now,
and help me speak those words
I need to say to know
what men who have gone before
have found worth passing back, frail
words whose weight
will lift us up, like flying buttresses
that hold stone years in place.

🍁 In the Third Month

First snow wet against the windshield.
I drive by the storefront where we found
his blue Toyota. How he loved that car—
put fur upon the dashboard to cover cracks—
then he and his girl devotedly stretched leather
across the back seat making a love nest.
And they went out to Western Auto and bought
a little fan, the kind bus drivers use,
and mounted it to blow down upon them
when they made love, parked by a roadside
or perhaps in one of those shadowed drive-ins.
It's a weekend and I'm about my errands,
Bach's *Sleepers Awake* on FM. The tears pour down
as I think how much he wanted to be a man,
simply a man with his woman and his car, later
his fireside books, those I still have,
saved too long to pass on—*The Way
of All Flesh, A Shropshire Lad, Don Quixote,*
and one stamped in gold but with all pages blank.

☙ Ghosts

Not ghosts but simply that forever
you won't quite know
there is not a presence where
you are yourself most in doubt
when passing near a place you sat
together, alert, and almost hearing
or when the old reality is near
in the thousand ways it will be.
And these days what is real
is not quite clear, or visible.
Let's say the ancient meanings
overlooked, runes that children carved,
are not so subtle as they were
in sky or stone or evergreen
and anywhere you walked together.

❦ At the Opera

I sit in the balcony,
next to an empty seat.
Three rows below me a man
slaps at his son,
for the small boy conducts
right along with the maestro,
waggles his head, jumps around
in his seat. I hold myself back,
sink into shadows, not wanting
to lecture anyone, to tell
the man what a privilege it is
to be present at the marriage
of Figaro, with his son,
nor go on to say it is also
rare privilege to share
in a life that's complete now,
a life I would like
to hear singing, conducting,
with hands I can only see
grabbing at stars, ancient fireflies.

🍁 First Snow

Hold it not a sin to regain your cheerfulness.
                              —KEATS, 1818

First snow. Much farther south we know
your grave is covered now, who were the song
and dance of my life. You had me laughing
till tears came. They tell me four more months
will bring some measure of relief, as if grief
times itself or can be like an ocean wave charted
in its journey out to sea, at last mingling
with billowing waters that somehow bring new life
by surface interchanging with the deep and dark.
They say that playful mist and dancing wave-tips
are found in abyssal bottoms where sharks
leave off, that journeys take the soul where God
alone, no mortal love, can follow—and that life
goes on, returns. On earth you made me see
rainbows in my life: I'd been blind before.
Out the window now I see across the roof the blue
gable that you painted, balanced in your tennis shoes,
bucket held and brush, your backward baseball cap
upon your head; thus you guaranteed that blue still
holding, signed on the corner shingle, a work of art.
In this world now we must at tiny blessings claw.

🍁 Sam

Trouble is, too common a type
and not just in art galleries
(at four he looked like a portrait
by Bronzino) or on the street
where I've watched him out of sight.
He is always in McDonald's,
football jacket, tow-headed.
One among a group in any
yard is Sam. I have all ages
now, like snapshots piled.
And swinging round
pole of a parking meter.
Sweeping up a restaurant,
part-time job. Football
in all seasons, practice lots,
on stage as Candide. (In life
it was Malvolio
he played on stage.) Again
and again learning
the hard lessons.
And older, what he'd have become.
Or younger, too well remembered,
nursing still, off
in the shadows, his mother
turned away for her weeping.

🍁 A Plastic Cube

Nothing but a paperweight, bright earth
within a cube of plastic, never whirling,
frozen till some bomb blasts
it to smithereens. By God, it's lovely,
this world stilled, with every country colored
the way it was in grade school
and continental arms that reach
around the poles as if to join
in peace, a hug that's meant to be eternal.
        Meridians divide
the seas as Aunt Ruth once split
a wondrous orange to slices. On such a scale
no grief looms large, no grave
can be discerned. From a distance,
say across a room, I see
this earth is one blue eye
mined in a crystal cave years and years
ago. The secret of its birth
requires a closer look, turning
such a numb cube end on end, not hot, not cold.
With worlds it's best
to let them serve and not inquire
too deeply what they're made of
or where their spinning takes us.

❧ Thanksgiving 1984

But headlong joy is ever on the wing.
　　　　　　　　　—MILTON

This year there will be no turkey
nor will you and your sisters sing that song
of grace around our table, grace abounding—
Evening has come, the board is spread.
Thanks be to God who gives us bread.
Our hands were joined and now I have
a red leaf only, maple you would tell me.
Sam, our sumacs are aflame again.
Like you they're loved through an open door.

🍁 The Weeping Session in Italy

I take your snapshot, the one where you're sitting
with a fishing pole, looking at me and laughing.
Now we're North of where we were together, quite a way,
on a lake you'd love, insist we should row right out on.
Mornings the waves ripple with wind, risky, but afternoons
they calm down. Sometimes, without you, we take a boat
much like the *vaporetto* you watched purr through Venice.
But it seems you're with me when I find a church, mountainside
stone set on a shelf, with a tall campanile that dares earthquakes.
Inside, there's a shadowed hush. My eyes adjust as I look up
at stained glass, at *bambini* with trumpets, angels that look
so much like you, surrounded by walls of cobalt blue. You were
an angel, Sam, and now I think of you as I light a candle,
gaze as if your spirit wavers there in flame, your soul.
On the side aisle they come and go, murmur bold confession.
There's a shelf of skulls, Christ reclayed upon some skeleton
dim-lit in glass. I cry a while, first heavy breath then tears
as if through rock cleft. No need to get the snapshot out.
Your portrait glows in mind and always will. I'll keep time free
for you each day. If weeping sessions help, worst dreams
may ease at last. Not long ago I dreamed you'd gone to war.
You had to crawl through fields of corn, our Civil War or one
you're spared from now. Amid dried stooks men stumbled, fired,
left corn as well as men cut down, and you. And then somehow
you reappeared, in World War I puttees and a little flat helmet
but this time I knew the war was dream. Pastel ladies laughed
from their touring car, their parasols unfurled, and the smoke
of battle made them sneeze—absurd. The dreams are rotten, Sam.
In only one you've come to me just as you were, great smile
to say you had just flown in. Most days we slog through war.
And when I leave some happy scene these days I say I'll be
right back, but then I lose that street, those friends. Is that
how it was with you, my son, the moon not light enough, death
out to grab the best he could that night? I would have flown

round earth to swoop you up and have you here with me
where we might mourn and light our candle for our choice
of uncles or that grandfather you so wept for, but not, my son,
                                        my son.

🍁 Brief Song

There will come a day
When you would have lived your life
All the way through,
Mine long gone.
And peace will descend then,
Such a great peace, like a breath
Moving those pines, moving
Even the stone.
And then, then I can let go.

🍁 Haiku

When wind blew my hair,
I felt like my son, smiling
and happy at last.

Bless the year too soon
and you'll repent for certain.
Watch it leave, then say.

"An outstanding Fall!"
a neighbor says, meaning well—
our golden sumacs.

All grief has structure
as tornadoes have centers,
wrapped in their rain shrouds.

That condolence card
had been signed "Love from us all"—
But not one came by.

Name on found granite—
friend that came forward, ready
to serve, through hard times.

My kiss on his brow—
Some men would not hug their sons,
much less this embrace.

Waking in the night,
the first thought always of him,
as if I could help.

Earth like black waters,
not a thought, settled again,
after taking all.

෬Laporte—buried there,
  yet for a month no one knew
  it simply means Door.

෬Best friend at his grave,
  sad to sense the soul's gone, yet
  he spoke through the snow.

෬Under the snow now,
  SAM carved on it, and dates, six-
  ty-five, eighty-four.

෬Out in mid-ocean
  there's a whitecap only we
  who loved him can see.

෬Your name, Samuel,
  means, *borrowed from God*—one boy
  lent to us, returned.

෬Banging to get in—
  dream about his birth—or word
  from the other world?

🍂 The Birth of Woe

Out of the pool, I did a little jump,
joyous, up and down, and thought,
"Now I am like my son Sam, happy, feeling
the good of the body." It was as if
he were inside me, and I joked
with the French grandmother with her two
small girls, both naked, the baby sitting
in a basket, the sister standing before
cypresses beyond—and the Mediterranean
farther out, blue and at peace. Down below
was the city of Nice, subject of Maupassant's
essay, which I had just read, up on the terrace
over the topless girls and the turquoise pool,
having my *café crème,* flipping the *Dictionnaire*
I had carried around twenty years. The essay
concerned the earthquake at Nice, in 1877.
Quel catastrophe! he had written, and yet
Nature had gone on with its sunrise, still
dawn over the sea as if nothing had happened.
And the Alps rosy-tinted above! And then
we went back to our mountainside shack
that reminded me of the cabin in Oregon
that summer Sam was our new babe and we bathed
him on the warped, rickety porch and his sister
held up the soap, above the wild river in flood.
Back at our table of planks above the blackberries
of France exactly like those near Coos Bay, I told you
how black I had felt that morning, lowest in years,
how I had made myself work, yet felt that something
had passed over, evil, brooding, life-threatening.
And then the girl came down with the message.
And I knew right away, knew from that moment.
Every omen made sense, even before we climbed
those terraced stones, up to the level of olives,
and the black phone merely confirmed word of woe,

how the dark one who had tried many times
had stolen our son. Signs fools could read
all made sense now, what I had known when I left him,
why I took *Dombey and Son* to read on the plane.
Then we traveled to kneel, wash blood off the stones.

🍁 Beads, Pony, Prayer

Dear Lord let us pray for another day
In which nothing happens, absolutely nothing.
I'm hardly back in shadows before my melted
Candle's droppings are brushed off
The glistening tray, to make still new—
Grief recycled just like life. Horses rear
Inside that tallow, and one horse my boy
Belovèd loved. He led him by a bridle
And rode him bareback, fed him hay and dappled
Apples. He left a watercolor of two stallions,
Both his fathers, he the third—that small pony—
I find him in all churches, caves, and ruins,
With other glowing angels, before dark widows
Who sit with sad eyes mumbling, snap-
Shot portraits cupped in hand or else
Those amber beads well-thumbed. "My will,"
One bead says, "Thy will" next, and never this
Duality gives way, nor all of me assent.

⚜ The Question

How long should I mourn?
Let me ask you, my son.
How long would you wish it?
Do you want it to go on?
Is there anything to be gained
for either of us, for both of us?
Are you so far away now
that you're no more than a wish,
the one I had on my mind
before you fulfilled it, came
quite early one morning
when mist was on fields
and we had slept there, waiting
in a tent for you, yet rushed
into the town, as if
a boy like you could not
have appeared out of the fields,
blue mists not far from the ocean.

🍁 Between Alp and Sea

I was preparing for the great blow
but did not know it, had simply driven
the old car up the mountain road, afraid
of the abyss all the time, thinking it was my
death that might come at any moment,
the fall, fire, the scorched body,
the hell of being alone. But safe
atop the mountain, I strolled the village,
had coffee in the Square, then found
a private ledge to view what stone age
man had waked to, many a dawn—blue valley
cut by river, silvered far below—
lazy scene at work, unmaking stone,
unmaking Alps, creating France.
And that stone age man,
out from his cave to squat, had left
clear word for me, along with the view
he loved. Prepare to abandon all,
he said, blue hills, the woman rubbed
till she gleams, and son you thought
safe over that sea, Oh happy happy son.

Vence, 1984

🍁 Regrets

Heaven knows we need never be
ashamed of our tears. —DICKENS

It had not happened to them,
the flower vendors, merchants, land-
lady, countess, tutor, chauffeur, maid,
old lady at her gate of black iron
with roses peeking through. It had not
happened to them, the people
on the road (red-haired woman
with her cane, resting on half
a crumbled wall—"No French today,"
I said, just waved half-
lifted hand). And not to swimmers
at the pool, tavern keeper, mistress
of the restaurant who saw in our bale-
eyes that it had happened, and not
to old wood chopper bald with hatchet
scar on scalp. To him I said "Revoir!"
And not to those with whom
we had to settle up accounts
in just one afternoon. In checking out
of Eden I was rough of hand,
grabbed change, allowed some rudeness
to lash out at clerks
and ticket takers, gatekeepers,
and most of all at flower girls
near stall I'd loved six weeks.
On the plane at last, Air France,
and climbing fast from paradise,
blue Riviera far below, a charming
coast, tears came. I was not ashamed
though they looked across the aisles
and back, and one peeked forward
from the chair behind though after lunch
they tended to their knitting, blue

skies to London, wooly clouds.
Year later I recall girl
in half-door open who offered
prayer hands raised to heaven, bronze
to last for years, turn to God one word

      REGRETS

with stone ribbon, one gilded
gleaming rose. To have bought it
would have been to know it truly happened
but I waved her back, took one
red rose, its stalk of thorns.

🍁 The Search

I had strolled bemused through a great
cemetery, tier upon tier, marble
slabs, tombs, exquisite angels
weathered, portraits in oval
like those on Grandfather's wall,
the sun beating on flowers
sealed forever in plastic or glass,
wreaths rotted away, fine wire
filigree left for the hero,
a soldier who had won the Legion
of Honor, a faded tricolor flag
for him too. I tried to imagine it—
something he did crawling
through mud on his knees, German
machine guns trained on him—or possibly
he flew one of those biplanes—wings
tipped bright as butterflies, not
a hint here on the tomb, just REGRETS,
a tricolor flag and many old
ribbons curled, unfurled, littering
the slab inside the iron fence, all his.
He had lived on, in the village of Vence,
through another war, and another.
I searched every face, faded portraits,
rubbed letters, and mud from a cross.
They do not weather well, these crosses
of iron, rusted away in a decade.
But I still could not find him.
Then I saw, above a wall made of tombs,
wife of the concierge, leaning far out
her high window, face toward the street,
great bosoms like bread loaves,
like Frieda's. "L'écrivain Anglais,
Lawrence, il est ici?" I called out.
"Non," she waved, turning briefly
away from her friend out there

somewhere beyond us, in the narrow
street of the village or at another
window. "Ils portent cet homme
à New Mexique! En Amérique!"
So they took him away, to America,
that frail little man, withered
and dried like a flower. But he had
been here, my friend, and that
was enough, to feel the ground sacred.
And not for two weeks would I know
I was already seeking my son, David indeed,
and would follow, back to America,
search for him, find the ground sacred.

Vence, 1984

🍁 In the Children's Library

Sam, retreating to find a room away
from murmurous girls, loud whispers,
music leaking from earphones while
midafternoon browsers of Sweet Briar lounge,
I come to the bright room kept for children, wonderful
books I did not read as a child. You
got through some of them and the novel
you started in the eighth grade reflected
your love of Tolkien and White and Farjeon,
and you loved *Black Beauty* at least
as much as equestrienne scholars here
who cross the campus in boots, jodhpurs,
cute little black jockey caps fastened at chin.
I sit by the window open to leaves falling,
now and then one upon the window ledge.
Oak tables are small and the squat chairs strong,
and I could have led you in, ten years ago
while you lived and there was much hope ahead.
Then I noticed a book propped, recommended—
You Come Too, with Frost's darkest poems inside,
those you copied out on a cypress root and
a birch slab, "Come In"—to the dark,
and "Dust of Snow"—as if from the pine
where you lie. I read them now,
these poems you so loved, lived and died by
and see that the book has been stamped "For grades
7, 8, and 9," as if an old man
reading and seeking your guidance and Frost's
were robbing the cradle of wisdom.
I read them for you, son who taught me to weep,
who taught me to say these prayers for the dark.

Virginia, 1985

✣ Writing

Basically the same—bad posture,
an unpainted chair, room far too cold.
But now no boy in his diapers can crawl
under the table, pull
himself up to the knob of the door,
say his first words, "Help me"
interrupting the poem, worthless,
and the father rising. Because he is up
and opens the door for his son
(only a door to a closet—blank
stucco walls with olivewood shelf)
he sees out the window the blue
and glittering-with-silver
Mediterranean. On the shore
an old man pitchforks seaweed
up to his cart. A bored mule waits.
Years later the boy calls again, "Help me,"
or so the fool father thinks. And he can't.

❧ Bhopal

I've often wondered how it is at times
Good people do what are as bad as crimes.
—CLOUGH

Eyes open, glazed like isinglass, the fire
behind gone out, this child of Bhopal lies
in his shallow grave of cinders—no time
for weeping as when we lost our son Sam
and stood, hands joined, to wish him well in some
life beyond. In fact he might have gone on
to Bhopal just in time to die again
at just three months. Not likely, but who knows?
One thing that's certain though is this: Third World
or one beyond, they're all our children now,
though borne by millions in brown arms and black,
and not much mourned by those who think their own
are wonders, others somehow less. And thus
I'll say good-bye to this son too, and yours.

🍁 The Parting

I knew it when we parted. —CLOUGH

That last hug haunts me, skull to skull,
father and son, *abrazo* as learned in Spain.
We stood in that room where you had slept
in the upper bunk, long gone now like that
aboard the *Ryndam* we sailed on when you were one,
your sister four. Where your nose touched
plaster wall a picture hangs now, an open
womb-door of stone, blue sky beyond. Once,
a decade older, you slept on a cot
in the corner, and we talked till midnight
as I did with my father on planks
down at the farmers' market just before dawn.
And in all you said I heard that understood
expectancy of life—so much to do, to learn—
such eagerness, tired ecstasy.
Now in an Italian church I ponder a shelf
of skulls. A cross-shape cut in glass
lets in dim light that they may be beheld,
all yellowed, hollowed, a school of bone.
But your dissolution, which I must bear,
is sudden falling snow of light, immense
and blinding, stunning blast that lasts for years.

🍁 And April Arrives

Rejoice a moment—then
Remember.
—MARY COLERIDGE

Sumac's velvet-branched, smooth
as moss to touch. White jonquils
join yellow daffodils. Blue jays
eat the seeds left out and when
they're gone, the big-pawed cat
sleeps on the concave slab
of our birdbath. The stripling pine
you helped me dig from mud
before we left that wood
has grown adult, sways in breeze,
last night lifted up a golden moon.
The tiny tree I claimed was birch
has blossomed, lovely as the old
fragmentary boughs found on Chinese scrolls.
It could well be brother to those
that stand so near you now, far north,
edge of a darksome wood. Sometimes
I almost see you, almost hear.
And yet there's emptiness to bear,
what Winter froze enraged by Spring.

Kansas City, 1985

74

🍁 To Sam

"God don't like ugly." And to
that would sometimes be added,
"And he cares very little for beauty."
—ROBERT HAYDEN

And if not for beauty like yours,
manly and charming, then what?
I was lulled by those years till I thought
you'd be given all earth could offer,
might make up for my sins, enlarge
on what gifts I had squandered, as if
you had been sprung from the gods.
Now I must struggle to do in your name
as I would have had you in mine, as if
I were you, and you the father long
mourned, whose spirit perhaps
makes the frail curtain flare
with light in the breeze.
And the old masks are empty.

❦ Tricks of the Mind

So take a firm grip on yourself as best
you can. —*The Epistle of Privy Counsel*

Use tricks of the mind, say the wise,
and I'm willing to try. Just say
it happened in the ancient days.
Pretend that he went with the Greeks
to their pagan kingdom, was perhaps
that green boy of stone who plays
his flute to this day on the terrace.
And think of scenes worse, those children
of Pompeii or Bhopal or Hiroshima.
Or here's a thought to consider:
He had a short life, but a good one,
and never partook of the evil.
And that's true. So one trick
of the mind may get through. And think
of those cheated of even more life,
how the gravedigger stood with his shovel
and said that his grandson lay near
but died at thirteen. And he leaned
on his shovel and wept, an old
gravedigger with no tricks of the mind.

🍁 Another Trick of the Mind

Out of a book, a little trick—
Instead of the picture and much longing
for that lost face,
place yourself within the frame.
You are back together again, if only
in the past or in the dream,
or this gilded picture in mind.
But it is no longer a dream or a picture
of loss. And then you go on,
down the road you have to go, together.

🍁 The Cypress Root

This was the taproot of a living cypress,
hollow where the life-force flowed through all those years,
and it is all you have left us.
I place it on end, pointing toward heaven now
the way you meant it, like a tusk
complete with round felt for not marring some surface.
But it is tough, this cypress root,
and could weather these elements—a hurricane
coming today—and yet I touch it with care,
like searching your face—a strange choice,
perhaps, for a boy—to carve out on a root
for his two fathers a poem of old Frost's,
"Come In," with its word of the light
dead in the West. You seemed
such a tough boy, strong always. But here
in a circle of bushes I can see
that everything about you was fragile,
face I saw for the last time, half-smiling voice
I heard for the last time. I place the root
so that I may again read the poem, see what
the message is, yours now
that the light has failed in the West.
You would like this place, the way
the spiders, crickets, a fly, all crawl
over the yellow letters fading,
read what they can of your writing. What
do you tell me of the dark we must face?
Do you summon me too? Is that why
the cowards with their taboos refuse to say
the names of their dead? Is that why they banish
fathers and sons from their dreams?
I carry the root up the road, feeling
the smooth hollows you left, shoulder blade,
strong back. It is like carrying your body,

looking down where Frost's words and yours
glow. You are warm in the sun.
I hold you between rows of the roots
and green glow of the tall yews clawing heaven.

🍁 The Return

The past and future were forgot
As they had been, and would be, not.—
But soon, the guardian angel gone,
The demon reassumed his throne
In my faint heart.   —SHELLEY

First visitation in a dream: you're back
with bags in hand, through screen door greeted.
And how did you make it back so fast, I ask.
You say you flew, got a ride from the airport.
So I think of that wondrous flight through skies,
snow blown in winds, great clouds tumbling, luminous,
and the landing as an angel might have it,
touching ground, then wobbling to steady himself.
Yet I fear that monster who gave you a ride.
What abduction was that, what crime on the way?
Still, I wake happy to have this small blessing.
And recall how at four you hugged the dark trees,
how you said you wanted to be born again, out of the corn.

🍁 The Petrified Forest

Practically everyone goes to the
Petrified Forest. — E. L. MAYO

And when it was time
I came to the Petrified Forest,
not of trees but men and women,
and I touched their cold faces.
I still had questions to ask,
and I told them of that grief
when I had lost them, no matter
how, their fault or mine (years
of that worthless emotion).
And I wondered again, aloud,
why we had made of our lives
such a stone hardness,
why so few of us held
to our roots, leafy with praise
one for the other, helping all
of us bear what we must come to.
And after a while I bent to the wind
to speak softly with petrified time.

Other books by David Ray

X-Rays: A Book of Poems
Dragging the Main and Other Poems
A Hill in Oklahoma
Gathering Firewood: New Poems and Selected
Enough of Flying: Poems Inspired by the Ghazals of Ghalib
The Mulberries of Mingo and Other Stories
The Farm in Calabria
The Tramp's Cup
The Touched Life
Not Far From the River
On Wednesday I Cleaned Out My Wallet
Elysium in the Halls of Hell

About the author

David Ray has won a number of awards for his writing, among them a Woursell Fellowship from the University of Vienna and the Woursell Foundation, the William Carlos Williams award of the Poetry Society of America for *The Tramp's Cup,* a National Endowment for the Arts Fellowship for fiction, and several PEN Syndicated Fiction Project awards for short stories. He is professor of English at the University of Missouri–Kansas City, where he has taught since 1971. In 1981–82 he was visiting professor at the University of Rajasthan, India and in 1987 taught as an exchange professor of English at the University of Otago in New Zealand.

Ray received his B.A. and M.A. from the University of Chicago. He is the author of ten books of poetry, including *Gathering Firewood: New Poems and Selected* (Wesleyan 1974), a book of short fiction, and a book of transcreations from the Prākrit. He was founding editor of *New Letters* magazine and creator of a weekly program for poetry heard on many National Public Radio stations. Ray lives in Kansas City, Missouri.

About the book

Sam's Book was composed in Granjon by Yankee Typesetters of Concord, New Hampshire. It was printed on 60lb. Glatfelter and bound by Malloy Lithographing, Inc. of Ann Arbor, Michigan. Design by Joyce Kachergis Book Design and Production, Inc. of Bynum, North Carolina.

Wesleyan University Press, 1987

0 00 02 0407294 6

MIDDLEBURY COLLEGE